Praying for Children

Praying Healing for Your Child

Ruth Hawkey

New Wine Press

New Wine Press
PO Box 17
Chichester
England PO20 6YB

ISBN: 1 874367 98 1

Typeset by CRB Associates, Reepham, Norfolk.
Printed in England by Clays Ltd, St Ives plc.

Contents

Preface

One of the greatest needs in our contemporary society, with its many fluctuations and modern problems, is for us to find a way of providing a stable and a secure environment for our children, as well as providing the facilities for healing for them, if that goes amiss. Now that most of us live in 'nuclear families' there does not seem to be the same support system for children that there used to be. At one time if a child in a family was in difficulty, an aunt, an uncle or loving grandparents would be aware of the problem and move in to help the child as best as they could.

Whilst this may not happen quite so much today, nevertheless it is very interesting to note that according to a report in *The Times* newspaper on Thursday May 8th 1997:

> 'Scientists have now realised what parents have always known: that grandmothers are indispensable to bringing up children! "Having children is risky and having a grandmother reduces the risk," Professor Kirkwood told a conference on ageing. "Grandmothers have experience and a valuable social role to play." '

It would seem therefore that even though the extended family is not as normal a feature of family life as it used to be, there is still a vital role for grandparents and other relatives to play in the life of a child in whatever form or to what extent that may be.

Because the family set-up is changing so rapidly these days, the church must be willing and also able to undergird the child's support system. Certainly they need to be very much aware of the kind of damage which children may be suffering from, as well as knowing how to pray intelligently into their problems and help them to walk into wholeness.

It is hoped that this book will be a help to those within the church who not only see the need to pray for children within their care, but also have a desire for further training so that they can pray intelligently. Parents, relatives, Sunday school teachers, secular teachers, youth workers and intercessors may also find it useful. It is an outcome of some seminars, which we have taught in various parts of the world on 'Praying Healing for our Children'. As we have submitted the teaching, people have asked us to offer it in written form for their future help and reference. I trust that you will find it beneficial.

Chapter 1

Foundations for Healing

Children can be delightful, naughty, exhilarating, frustrating little people as well as diminutive angels or tiny devils, depending on the time of day, their state of mind or whether their parents have the patience of Job or have run out of steam!

Children are also, on the whole, without guile. One little boy who was in my school class, and who was six years old, inquired anxiously of me as to whether I was tired or not? Thinking he was such a kind and observant child, I quickly slipped into self-pity and said in rather a miserable voice, 'Yes I am tired Daniel. How did you know?' His reply took me somewhat by surprise; 'It's because your eyes are all red and blotchy Miss.' Needless to say the day took a downward turn from that moment on! Another child came to my desk one morning and told me that I was smelling beautiful. Struggling desperately to think whether I had put any perfume on that morning, I replied faintly, 'Oh thank you Jack. That's very kind of you.' 'Yes' he said, 'You smell just like a ripe banana!'

According to the Scriptures, children are described as gifts from God, to their parents, to their wider families and to the church.

'These are the children which God has graciously given.'
(Genesis 33:5)

As gifts therefore they are meant to be received joyfully and to be treasured for who they are, as well as being treated very carefully and with a great sense of responsibility. Children are also described as a heritage:

> *'Sons are a heritage from the Lord.'*   (Psalm 127:3)

As well as an old man's crown!

> *'Children's children are a crown to the aged.'*
> (Proverbs 17:6)

You only have to observe a doting grandfather dangling his three-year-old grandchild upon his knee, to see the truth of that statement!

In God's perfect plan He designed a safe and a secure family structure, which would give to a child the protection, the confidence and the security which he would need in order to grow and develop in the way God intended him to. His intention was to form a strong godly bonding between the parents and the child and the umbilical cord would be symbolic of this. This cord and the bonding it represents were meant to feed good things into the child even within the womb. The godly bonding would then continue to nourish and cherish the child in the unique family relationship into which they had been placed.

Some of the nourishing and the cherishing which the Heavenly Father intended would include the following: a deep sense of security in which the child could experiment and develop without a fear of failure or punishment, and an acceptance of their intrinsic worth and value. An unspoken recognition that 'You are special because you are who you are; simply because you are you, a part of our family.' God intended that the child would be continually fed encouragement and affirmation: 'You did well, I like the way you did that.' 'Well done. You are such a blessing to us.'

Children have a number of basic needs, two of which are the need for love and the need for a sense of significance.

They need the inner knowledge that they are intrinsically worth a great deal to the parents to whom they have been entrusted. On the whole the mother meets the child's need for love, whilst the father meets its need for significance, although both, to a greater or lesser extent, will be inputting both of these strands. It is significant that according to the Scriptures, a husband is meant to meet the wife's need for love: 'Husbands love your wives' and wives are to meet their husbands need for significance, honour and respect: 'Wives honour your husbands.' As mothers and fathers they then pass these good things, which they have received from each other, onto their children.

From the moment of conception the character of God is written into the spirit of the child, for God was involved in its creation. It says in Psalm 139:13:

> *'You created my inmost being; you knit me together in my mother's womb.'*

Two important questions would seem to be:
- How is the character of God developed within a child as it grows?
- Where do children get their image of God?

The answer to both questions to a greater or a lesser extent is that they develop a picture of God from their parents, and especially from their father. Therefore a father's input is vital. *Leading Lads*, a study compiled by the charity **Young Voice**, shows that a male role model is vital to a child's self esteem and confidence. They interviewed 1,400 boys aged between thirteen and nineteen and found that fathers still play a key role in their son's lives. The three qualities of a father which they found to be most helpful were:
- making time for children,
- being prepared to talk through their problems, and
- showing an interest in their work.

The picture of the Heavenly Father, which their earthly father inputs, will either be a true reflection or a distorted image. For example, if a child's father is away from home a good deal, or he has to work very long hours, a child may get the impression that God is never available or accessible to him. Unfortunately pastors, doctors, seamen etc., can come into this category. Sometimes because of his job, a father may have to withdraw into his study or office on an evening and at weekends, and this will add to a child's belief that Father God is a long-distance God who is difficult to approach.

It may be that a child has a very strict father, one who was very similar to a lady we prayed for who had a sergeant major for a dad. At six years old she had to keep her bedroom as neat as the proverbial parade ground, for nothing had to be out of place. Friday evening was an especially traumatic time for her, for that was the night when her room and her person were inspected! She grew up believing that God had a similar personality; one who would look you over and judge you on a regular basis, and who had to be placated at all costs.

If a child is unfortunate enough to have an abusive father, that will have all kinds of repercussions in the image a child has of God. Hidden somewhere in the subconscious will be the belief that no matter how nice God may seem, somewhere along the line He will eventually abuse you. On the other hand a child may be raised by a father who gives the child mixed messages, like a Pastor's daughter I prayed with, who saw her father as a great evangelist in the church but as a man who beat her mother at home. This implanted in her a great distrust of Father God. Her big question was, 'Can God be trusted, or will He also prove to be a hypocrite like my dad?'

If the image of God taken from their earthly father clashes with the image of God which was written in their spirit at the time of conception, the child will most likely turn away from the true picture of God and trust the earthly image which the birth father has provided. The story of the Prodigal Son is very useful in helping children to develop a true picture of what God is like, but we need to be aware that it can take time to replace that which has been erroneously fed in. Jesus in this beautiful story paints a picture of the Father as being

10

gracious, generous, loving, wise, forgiving, accepting, and approachable. Of course we can always point to the fact that Jesus Himself claimed that if we have seen Him, we have seen the Father.

Another important area that any child needs to experience is that of being nurtured and cherished and this is primarily the role of the mother. The story of Solomon and the two women who argued over whose baby was still alive is a very interesting one. True mothers will always lay down their own needs in order to nurture and meet the demands of their children and we see this reflected in this story recorded in 1 Kings 3:16–28.

Children fed at their mother's breast will receive there the love and the emotional nurturing which they require, as well as the milk which they need in order to develop physically. Held in the safety of a mother's arms a child will be fed and satisfied physically, whilst at the same time receiving the loving nourishment which God intended. Arms are meant to hold and not to push away.

A child, of course, has a primary need for his body to be provided for. Amongst other things it needs food, drink, rest, activity, exercise, hobbies, clothing, touches and hugs. It has been said that 'Lack of mothering endangers the infant's mental health and threatens his very survival.' So in summary a child is meant to receive:

- **Security**: 'This is a safe place for you to be yourself. We will always be here for you.'
- **Love**: 'We love you.'
- **Self-worth**: 'You are worth a great deal to us; it does not depend on what you do.'
- **Acceptance**: 'We accept you, as you are; your shape, your size and your abilities.'
- **Encouragement**: 'You can do it; we think that you are wonderful.'
- **Value**: 'We value you for who you are.'

As well as giving the child physical and emotional nurture, he also needs to be fed spiritually. We read in Luke 1:80 where Dr Luke speaking about John the Baptist says that, *'the child grew and became strong in spirit;'* and in Luke 2:52 we are told that *'Jesus grew in wisdom and stature.'* Children need spiritual as well as emotional and physical nurture, but the question would seem to be: 'How do you nurture a child's spirit?' The good news is that good parents, relatives and teachers all do it naturally. They automatically clap their hands in delight when their child achieves something; their words of approval go straight into the child's spirit. They speak the truth of God's word into them and they make sure that there are times of true creativity for the child to move into: music, art, and exploration of the world around them. They continually find ways to build up, rather than tear down, the child's self-esteem.

Maybe this is a good place to mention **Covering**. God's plan and purpose is that a child will have the security of knowing and feeling itself protected, especially through its early years, for a child's spirit is very sensitive, open and vulnerable at this formative time. In order for that to happen it needs a godly covering. A lady whose father died in the war grew up with great fears. The Holy Spirit showed her that when her father died she had lost her protection and this resulted in great fear and panic attacks, which continued into her adult years.

There is no greater need in childhood than knowing a father's protection and if this is missing or inadequate the child may possibly grow up to be very insecure, fearful and anxious. One young girl, whose father had abandoned her when she was five years old, developed into a teenager who was very vulnerable and insecure. Her life was overwhelmed with fears and anxieties which were eventually traced back to the loss of the protection of her father at a very vulnerable age.

Covering by a parent is especially important in the spiritual area until the child individuates. According to 1 Corinthians 7:14:

> *'The unbelieving husband has been sanctified through his wife, and the unbelieving wife has been sanctified through her*

> *believing husband. Otherwise your children would be unclean, but as it is, they are holy.'*

However there comes a time when a parent will need to release their child into maturity. Again the story of the Prodigal Son can be most helpful for it is often a very difficult thing for a parent to do. Free-will is a very precious gift, which is God-given, and there inevitably comes a time when a child must individuate and go their own way and follow their own path.

As well as godly nurture a child needs godly discipline in order to grow and develop in a positive way and the book of Proverbs gives parents much advice in this sphere.

Proverbs 22:6 says that we are to,

> *'Train a child in the way he should go, and when he is old he will not turn from it.'*

Whilst Proverbs 13:24 affirms that:

> *'He who spares the rod hates his son, but he who loves him is careful to discipline him.'*

Proverbs 29:15 also says that:

> *'The rod of correction imparts wisdom, but a child left to himself disgraces his mother.'*

It is important to remember that godly discipline and correction are necessary, not in order to break the will, but rather so that such discipline will be used to train and bend the will into God's ways. It is also crucial to remember that unconditional love is the basis of any good discipline.

A wise parent will understand and take into account a child's temperament in this area of discipline and training for there is a need to discern what motivates each individual child and to use discipline accordingly. Training and teaching a child in the way which is appropriate to the temperament of that child is important, for some are much more sensitive than others.

According to Romans 12:3–9 it could be argued that just as God places a basic inward drive in each adult person, so He implants a primary motivation within each child. This passage talks about the seven motivational gifts: prophecy, serving, teaching, exhorting, giving, administration, and showing mercy. It is important to discern what is the motivational gift of the child, and in the area of discipline to work with them in their gifting.

The child's spirit can be sorely wounded if the parent disciplines harshly without understanding the temperamental nature of the child. For example, if the child's motivational gift is that of 'sensitive mercy', then the child can be deeply wounded by harsh scolding or excessive spanking.

Glenn Clark, a great teacher in the area of prayer, affirms that each child comes into the world with 'sealed orders'. Every human being has a unique destiny to fulfil and part of the calling of a parent is that they will help each child to 'unseal his own special orders'; to discover what it is that he is meant to be and to do. We are to train up the child in the way that **he/she** should go, for each child is formed differently and is unique in character.

According to Harold Dewberry in his book *One Plus One Equals Three*, which I have found very helpful indeed on this subject of discipline, there are three levels to be observed:

- instruction,
- warning, and
- correction.

The first level is **instruction**. A child needs specific instructions as to what is, and what is not, allowable. There are two kinds of instruction; that of example and that of specific teaching. Parents, Sunday school teachers and grandparents are all-important examples to a child. What you are, will speak louder to them than any words which you speak. The power of example through a parent does more to train the child than any other single thing. If a child sees that there is a real sense of respect between husband and wife then, without words, the child is being taught to respect others.

However, sometimes it is necessary to give a child specific instructions in order to teach the child the difference between what is right and wrong and what is allowable and what is not. He will need good standards to live by; to know what is acceptable or unacceptable behaviour. It is important to establish a right attitude in his heart, and to do this, it is very helpful to share and communicate on a friendship level. It may take time and patience to specifically explain to the child what you expect from them in certain situations, but it is absolutely essential and well worth the time and effort.

A child will need instruction in many practical matters (how to set tables, tie shoelaces etc.). He will also need to know what is expected of him concerning moral values: truthfulness, respect etc., In this area it is very likely that we may need to spell out what we expect from them. This is where boundaries and rules come in. There are three particular areas in which a child will need specific instruction: obedience, respect and responsibility.

The second level of discipline is that of **warning** the child when he is stepping outside of the boundaries which have been agreed. If, for example, a child has decided to go against your example and instruction, then it is only fair to give him a clear warning, which is best and most effective if it appeals to the child's conscience. Some questions which we will need to ask ourselves, are:

- 'Were my instructions clear?'
- 'Was he simply being childish or was he being rebellious?'
- 'Was he reacting to me personally?'
- 'Did I wound his feelings and cause him to react out of his pain or anger?'

A child should be warned only once and then corrected, otherwise in the future the warning will probably go unheeded.

The third level is that of **correction**. As we have already seen, the book of Proverbs is the one book in the Bible that speaks the most about using discipline as a means of correction. However, the way and the attitude in which we correct a child is vitally important for future relationships within the family. There needs, if possible, to be an acknowledgement of responsibility by the child for stepping outside of the boundaries. He should not be corrected in public if at all possible, for to humiliate and embarrass a child in front of others is definitely not godly. It is also necessary not to over-correct the child and to take care to comfort them after each correction.

According to Scripture, foolishness is bound up in the heart of the child and godly discipline and correction are not meant to break the spirit and the will, but rather to train them and to bend them into God's ways. In 1 Kings 1:6 we read that King David did not discipline Adonijah:

> *'His father had never interfered with him by asking, "Why do you behave as you do?" '*

This would seem to have been to the detriment of the man! True discipline is walking in the way of the Father:

> *'For you know that we dealt with each of you as a father deals with his own children.'*   (1 Thessalonians 2:11–12)

So we can see the importance of the father and the mother's role in nurturing and feeding the child's spirit, soul and body, and applying the correct discipline to him whenever that is required. Thus he will be raised in the way that God desires and plans, and grow and develop into the person God intended him to be.

However, Satan is always at work to spoil God's plans for the family. He deceived Adam and Eve and they sinned, and God cursed Satan and said in Genesis 3:15:

> *'I will put enmity between you and the woman, and between your offspring and hers; he will crush your head, and you will strike his heel.'*

Since that moment, Satan's plan has been to destroy the children of promise in order that this curse of God should not be fulfilled. Thus he schemes to steal, kill, deceive, bind and destroy our children. Jesus says that Satan was a murderer from the beginning and we are told that it was Satan who was behind the first murder of Abel by Cain. In Genesis 4:7 God warns Cain, *'sin is crouching at your door.'* Satan actually took both of Adam and Eve's children, one by death and the other by separation and curse.

We can also see the hand of Satan behind the murder of the Hebrew babies. Exodus 1:16 says:

'When you help the Hebrew women in childbirth and observe them on the delivery stool, if it is a boy, kill him; but if it is a girl, let her live.'

Satan was undoubtedly behind the attempt on the life of Moses as a baby, and also the life of Joseph, when he used his brothers to try and destroy him. 2 Kings 11 tells the story of Athaliah, the daughter of Jezebel, who was motivated by Satan to kill her grandchildren. We read that only Joash was saved. If we consider the life of Jesus we see that Satan frequently tried to kill Him. For example, shortly after His birth through Herod the King, and then again later by the Pharisees and Sadducees who tried to stone Him to death.

The threat of 'crushing Satan's head' widened that day on Calvary, for all Christians are part of the 'Seed' of Jesus:

'Then the dragon was enraged at the woman, and went off to make war against the rest of her offspring – those who obey God's commandments and hold the testimony of Jesus.'
(Revelation 12:17)

Thankfully we have the promise of God in Romans 16:20 that:

'The God of peace will soon crush Satan under your feet.'

Some people see Satan as being behind the present increase in abortions and the abuse of children in our present day, for he is always seeking to destroy God's plans and purposes. He seeks to destroy the family structure; to lead our children into rebellion; to rob them of good nurturing; to steal the child's innocence and to spoil the parent's protection.

Chapter 2

Roots of Damage

There are many reasons as to why children become hurt, damaged and wounded throughout their lives, and we will consider some of them in this chapter.

Sins of the parents in parenting

A parent, by not providing the godly covering, nurture and discipline which God intended, can either knowingly or unknowingly inflict hurt and damage on their child. For example, one parent was known to frequently steal from his child, continually raiding his piggy bank so that he would have money for drink or cigarettes, thus causing the child to feel deep anger towards his father. To lie to a child can also cause irreparable damage, especially if it is repeated again and again. We all make mistakes **but** some parents deliberately sin against their children. This can take the form of any kind of abuse or neglect as well as inflicting wilful physical damage upon them.

Learned behaviour

In this area of parent's sinning against a child, learned behaviour is a very strong force. A child who sees his parents sinning may assume that if is all right for them, then it is all right for him. If a child is made to 'tell them I'm not in,' whether that be the milkman for his bill, or some friends coming to call, it would teach the child that it is all right for him to tell little white lies also. Sometimes this can have serious consequences. We would call this the absorption process. Scripture highlights the important influence an atmosphere has upon a child. 1 Kings 15:11 and 26 tell of the different atmospheres which Asa and Nadab imbibed:

> *'Asa did what was right in the eyes of the Lord, as his father David had done.'*

Whilst Nadab:

> *'...did evil in the eyes of the Lord, walking in the ways of his father and in his sin.'*

In this sphere of example, grandparents are very important figures to the little child, and they too need to be careful as to what the child is learning from their lifestyle and from their behaviour.

Sins of the child

There is original sin in all of us and that includes in our children too, whether we want to see it or not! It seems impossible that the sweet little baby, who is the image of his dad, is also in like manner, a sinner like his father. Just try saying 'no' to him when he comes to an age of understanding and you will soon realise that yes, that small innocent baby has the same problems as the rest of us!

Sins of others

There is a strong possibility that other people will inflict hurt upon our children some time in their lives, either intentionally or by mischance. Hopefully this will be minimal and repairable, unlike the damage inflicted on the teenage girl I ministered to, whose uncle had abused her. Or like the young girl who used to baby-sit for a Christian couple, because they were friends of her adoptive parents. Unfortunately on her visits to their house the husband abused her frequently, and she reasoned to herself that it was because she had been adopted. It was the only way that she could make sense of the situation, otherwise why did her adoptive parents allow it?

Other authority figures can also inflict harm. For example, those in a position of *loco parentis* like teachers, or even ministers. One very bright child suffered for years with the belief that he was stupid because his teacher had labelled him a failure at the age of six! If 'Miss' said it then it must be true.

Television and computers have the potential for good or evil in the life of a child. Violence on the screen, some cartoons, toys, games, or children's books all need to be vetted by the wise and discerning parent. There are some computer games, such as 'Dungeon and Dragons', which could inflict serious harm on a sensitive or even a not-so-sensitive child. One such game, based on Jurassic Park, features humans being eaten by dinosaurs as blood splashes and screams echo. Parents need to be aware of what children may be watching in their bedrooms.

Sins of the ancestors

John Eddison in his book *Understanding Leadership* says, 'the proper time to influence the character of a child is about one hundred years before it is born.' Our family line definitely has an influence upon the lives of our children, either for good or for ill. The fact that family sin, weaknesses and behaviour patterns can each have consequences in the life of a child is a well-known fact, especially in the secular world. They see that children suffer from the consequences of addictions, abuse, and adultery within the family line, as well as very often going on (although not always) to propagate the same patterns in their own families. Scripture calls this generational sin (Exodus 20:5; Leviticus 26:39–40.) Suffice it to say that occult sin, false religion, sexual sins, addictions, fears, phobias, and ancestor worship, can all pass down the family line, and many a child is walking in the consequences of the sins of their fathers. We do not have the space to teach into this area too deeply, but for a fuller treatment of this subject I would recommend my book *Freedom from Generational Sin.*

Trauma and stress

Traumas both before and after birth can result in deep wounding within the spirit of a child. For example, if a mother has had previous miscarriages there is a strong possibility that her fears for the present baby will be picked up by the child in the womb. Scientists now believe that a baby, from a very early age whilst in the womb, can tune in to its parent's feelings and other outside influences. One lady, whose husband had a serious car accident whilst she was six months pregnant, found that her child was subsequently overly nervous about travel. 'Take care' was her frequent warning to other members of the family who were going on simple journeys, and she worried incessantly until they returned. She had no knowledge of her mother's feelings whilst she was a child in the womb but had undoubtedly picked up on her mother's fears.

An attempted abortion will also result in impacting a baby in the womb and such a child may suffer from frequent illnesses. Some have even been known to attempt suicide in a similar manner to the attempted abortion. For example, if the mother took pills, the suicide attempt will be by pill-taking. If a child's parent dies whilst they are at a relatively young age, there may grow within the child an expectation of future abandonment, which they will then almost seek to pursue.

Much damage can also result from varied traumas throughout life, such as unfortunate accidents or intentional harm, as happened in one horrific incident concerning a little girl who watched her father batter her mother to death.

Another child was terrified of water, and it transpired as he shared it, that when he was two he had almost drowned in a garden pool.

In this area of trauma, **sexual abuse** perhaps goes the deepest, for it is a primary cause of bringing deep damage to the inner being of a child and it can bring about a state of total confusion. There is often an ambivalence of feelings towards the abuser because the child usually knows them. Guilt, fear, anger, and shame are some of the conflicting emotions, which often lead to the child developing a crushed or a broken spirit. When I inquired of one young girl what was the primary emotion which she felt with regard to the abuse, she swiftly replied: 'dirty, I feel dirty.'

Stress

According to a report in *The Times* it was very rare for children to suffer from stress and anxiety a generation ago, but in modern times more and more children appear to be in misery. In fact, children as young as eight are battling with severe anxiety. Peter Wilson, a child psychotherapist and director of the children's mental health charity **Young Minds**, is reported as saying in *The Times* newspaper that:

'We are seeing increasing numbers of children suffering from what would be termed severe states of turmoil, agitation and disequilibrium. They are suffering from extreme worry about themselves and their families, manifesting in depression, extremely disruptive behaviour, violence against either themselves or others, drug abuse or attempted suicide.'

We in the church need to be aware of the needs of such children. We need to know the best ways to support the families, as well as finding the keys to praying for them.

Rejection

Rejection at any stage of life can be deeply disturbing but it is especially so in the tender years of early childhood. Rejection can take root within the spirit of the child, as early as at the time of conception. For instance, if the child was conceived during a rape situation, or in an atmosphere of deep anger, then at the very moment it was intended to feel acceptance and joy, there will be fear and rejection instead.

The birth period is also very important, in that the child's spirit is very sensitive to the atmosphere surrounding its birth. It may be that the baby that is born is a girl, when the father was desperate for a boy, and in his spirit the father rejects her. The child, because of the inevitable bonding between father and child, will pick this up in her spirit and will react accordingly. Any future rejections at school, by teachers or by their peer group, will tend to seal the rejection in even more deeply.

Speaking death to their spirits

Some authority figures actually speak death into a child's spirit rather than the life which God intended. Teachers, parents, pastors, and Sunday school teachers all have this ability because they have an open entrance into the heart of a child. Proverbs 18:21 speaks of death and life being in the power of the tongue, and many a person has used their tongue and this power in order to belittle and wound a child in a lasting way. To say to a little one: 'You're no good,' 'You'll never amount to anything,' 'No one will ever want to marry you,' or some other such wounding words, will inflict a deep and a long-lasting pain.

Chapter 3

Results of Damage

Spirit, soul and body

Because children are formed and shaped in the same manner as an adult, they are thus created spirit, soul and body. Therefore, whatever happens in one area of their being will have an out-working in other areas. For example, if a child suffers physically it will undoubtedly have repercussions in all of the other areas of his being: emotionally, spiritually, volitionally and mentally.

A child may suffer from physical neglect and abuse and this will probably result in his becoming very confused in his thinking. Questions such as: 'Why are they hurting me?' 'I love my mum and dad, why do they keep hitting me?' 'What have I done to make them hate me?' will continually be raised in his mind, and will no doubt cause deep confusion in his spirit.

Obsessive behaviour or anxious patterns of thought may overcome children. It may be that they will become driven by fear. It has been said that 90% of children have some fear or fears. With three-year-olds it is often a fear of dogs, with four-year-olds it is often a fear of the dark. These fears may be many and varied depending on what has happened. A little girl, whose father had died when she was young, became very fearful of any rows between her mother and subsequent stepfather. She was convinced that if they argued and fought, she would lose him too, so when she was put to bed in the evening, she would listen to their conversation downstairs, whilst sitting on the stairs. If he was whistling it meant that he was happy and he wouldn't leave, so she could safely go to bed and to sleep. However, if they were arguing she had to stay awake until her parents eventually came to bed themselves. Needless to say her schoolwork suffered tremendously.

As well as suffering in the mind and the emotions, a child may have secondary damage in their will. For example, they may be unable to make decisions for themselves, or become very rebellious. They may get into drugs or promiscuous behaviour. They may even take on shame, guilt, and inadequacy, which may then manifest as deep anger, or conversely they may become strongly dependent upon the parent, depending upon the nature of the child. If there is a persistent clashing of the wills of the parents and the child, this can do tremendous harm in the child's spirit.

As well as damage in the soul (the mind, emotions and will), there will most likely be damage in the child's spirit. Any lack of spiritual input and tactile affection will lead to starvation of the spirit. A little five-year-old girl who was adopted by 'emotionally cold parents' frequently snuggled up to her teacher at story-time for the spiritual input which she was lacking. Fortunately the teacher had the wisdom to realise what was happening and reacted accordingly. I give a fuller exposition on the work and damage to the human spirit, in my book *Healing the Human Spirit*.

Sometimes a child will feel physical pain in his or her body, which has occurred as an outworking of pain from the soul or the spirit area. As we have seen, as people we are one, and what happens in any particular area of our being will have an effect on the other parts. Maybe a child will complain of a stomach-ache, and her mother will dutifully take her along to the doctors who find nothing wrong with her. Only later may they discover that she was being bullied incessantly by her peer group at school.

It may be that a teenager will begin to lose weight quite drastically and develop anorexia or bulimia. The question must always be 'What is causing the physical problem?' One girl when she was five years old was forced to eat rice pudding by her father, even though it was making her sick at the time. She suffered from deep feelings of anger and shame against her father and kept these buried for years. Eventually she developed bulimia in her teens, another instance of the emotional having an effect on the physical.

Another physical reaction to emotional pain is that of nail-biting or trembling, jingling coins or tapping of the fingers, etc. Very often such actions are linked with trying to keep the damaged emotions under control. One boy who had been badly rejected as a baby spent a lot of the time tapping his foot incessantly while he watched television. One little girl refused to speak to adults after some physical abuse at home. She would converse with her peer group, but ignored all attempts by the teacher to have a conversation with her. It was only after many months that a small break-through was made, and she began to share hesitatingly with a kind and loving dinner lady.

Recurring behaviour patterns

Stealing

There are many reasons for a child beginning to **steal** from others, and it is necessary to find out what is the root of the thieving, which as we will see, may be due to many and varied reasons. For example, a child may be stealing because he is feeling very insecure and scared, or he may be trying to gain acceptance through his stealing. One young boy used to regularly enter a sweet factory on a Friday evening. He stole sweets and gave them to his friends the following week at school, because he was trying to buy friendship through his stealing. It is interesting to note that he never ate any of the stolen sweets himself. That was part of his moral code!

Someone has said that a child may steal because he has been stolen from, and this too can be a reason for a child's thieving behaviour. He is hitting back, albeit often sub-consciously, for what the world has done to him. Stealing can also be a form of punishment against the parents: a child getting their own back on a perceived ill. On the other hand it may be an inherited weakness coming down the family line, or maybe they have seen their parents steal and they have learnt to copy such sinful behaviour. It may also, of course, be due to the child's own sinful greed, in other words a result of original sin.

Self-mutilation

Some children will cut or inflict other damage upon them-selves due to low self-esteem or rejection. This can happen in any stage of a child's life, although often it manifests itself in the teen years. This is probably due to the intense pressure often surrounding this stage in life, due to examinations or to the change in hormones. One boy, from a well-adjusted Christian family home, resorted to cutting himself due to a number of factors, the main one being an inner drive to perfectionism in the examination system.

Bed-wetting

Before looking for any hidden roots as to why the child has begun to wet the bed, it is important to check out the physical side first. It may simply be a urinary disorder which needs medical attention, and the doctor should be the first port of call. Conversely a child may be wetting the bed because of their repressed feelings. Maybe they have stored up a lot of anger, guilt or shame and if they are unable to, or are not allowed to express themselves throughout the day, then during the night the unconscious will take over, in which case the result may be to wet the bed. They may have the body of a twelve-year-old child but the emotions of a two-year-old and when they fall asleep they begin to express themselves as a two-year-old again. If they don't get to the toilet in time, the result is a wet bed.

The child may wet the bed through fear. Traumas, abuse, and deprivation can all cause the child to have nightmares, and the body will respond in fear and maybe result in bed-wetting. It is important not to make a big issue of this. One little girl was made to wash the sheets every morning before she went to school, which left her no time at all to wash herself. As you can imagine she was teased mercilessly at school for the fact that she had a terrible smell.

We must always ask the reason behind the behaviour of the children we are dealing with, because these can vary enormously. If a child wets himself at school, it is vital that the teacher has understanding and sympathy, otherwise the embarrassment and the shame can go very deep, and become long lasting.

Over-dependence

If a child is showing an over-dependence on an adult it may mean that there is a sense of deep insecurity in its spirit. The 'don't leave me' syndrome can be out of fear as well as out of insecurity. One little girl cried for six months on being left at nursery school by her mother, and on reflection it was felt that this was due to her having been rejected at birth (admitted by the mother), and a fear of further rejection settling in. Sometimes the child will have picked up on the fear of the mother who has difficulty allowing the child out of her sight, in which case you will need to pray for the mother as well as the child.

Bullying

Sometimes you may be confronted by a child, either your own or one you are called upon to pray for, who is bullying other children. It is helpful and necessary to understand why a child resorts to picking on other children, for it is an undoubted fact that the bully needs help too. Often a tough guy has a low self-image and they will take out their frustrations on their peers. They have the outer image of toughness but the inner knowledge of weakness. For example, a child **may** bully because his parents or other siblings are bullying him, so maybe he then reacts by trying to get control over someone else. Sometimes parents are very strict and controlling and the child will lash out at others in a pecking order in order to prove his ability to fight his corner, away from his parents.

On the other side it is possible to get a child with a victim spirit; one who experiences the terrifying side of being bullied; one who is always being picked on. This may be due to generational issues, a familiar victim spirit coming down the family line, or to present-day traumas, such as abuse in the early years. For such children it is almost as though they have a notice hung around their necks saying: 'I have been abused, please keep hurting me.'

According to **Kidscape**, an organisation concerned with children who have been bullied, they say that the majority of bullying takes place in the lunch hour and it is important that parents, guardians and teachers all look out for obvious signs.

Signs to look out for
There may develop within the child a fear of going to school on their own. Whereas usually they have been quite content to walk to school, suddenly they want a lift, or for mum or dad to accompany them on a morning and meet them in the evening. The child may begin to do poorly in their school-work or to regularly have their schoolbooks or their clothes torn. Another indication could be that the child begins to return home starving because they have had their dinner money stolen. They may become very withdrawn or tearful and have unexplained scratches and bruises. It may be in this context that they start to wet the bed or to have nightmares.

Irrational behaviour

Withdrawal is a form of irrational behaviour that will often have a rational explanation. Some children may in fact become so badly withdrawn that they begin to live in a dream world. Parents of such children often become very anxious and fortunately seek help for them. Needless to say in order to bring healing, it is necessary to find out the source of the problem. One normal, happy, contented little boy spent most of his days in nursery school, painting beautiful coloured pictures, talking about them animatedly to his teachers. One day he took a black paintbrush and began to go over his beautiful coloured paintings with black paint. The obvious question the teachers asked themselves and his mum and dad, was why this was happening. It transpired that his favourite granny had just died and this was his way of expressing his inexpressible grief. He was so withdrawn that he refused to talk about the death to his teacher or to his parents but he used his paintings as his safety outlet. Eventually once the cause of his behaviour was known, the teachers were able to gradually draw him out and his pain was safely expressed.

Another form of irrational behaviour is that a child may make responses which are totally inappropriate to the situation in hand. For example, they may laugh and cry in the wrong place and at the wrong time. One young girl used to smile and laugh whilst relating to us how she was sexually abused by her brother and his friends. On asking her to describe the reason why she laughed, she shared with us that when the abuse was taking place they had insisted that she join in and laugh with them or they would make it even worse. Even though she hated what they were doing to her, nevertheless out of her fear, she would smile and laugh as best she could. This had become a pattern of behaviour which she found difficult to break.

Obsessive behaviour, such as spelling words in the middle of a sentence, or counting the cracks in a pavement, can also be irrational and uncontrollable. One young child developed the disturbing habit of compulsively having to sound out words in a sentence that he was forming. It began shortly after starting school. For example he would say 'Hello, my name is SAM, what is your NAME?' spelling out the words in capital letters. It transpired that starting school and consequently the learning environment had been so traumatic for him that this was his way of trying to cope with and control the situation.

Some children suffer from the very difficult condition known as autism. It has been estimated that, at the last count, there were at least 73,600 children with autism and related disorders in England and only 3,300 special places available for them to receive help. At the present time there is no known reason or cure for this distressing condition but it may be that this disorder is due to a chemical imbalance. Sometimes we have not got the key to healing, and all we can do is go to the Lord and intercede on behalf of the child and his parents.

Lying

Experts insist that children are not born liars, but that they have learned from their parents, teachers and friends that it pays to tell lies. This may be true, but it seems a very pat answer and certainly will not be true in every case. Again we need to ask the question as to why the child has resorted to telling lies. For example, it may be that they are seeking to deceive because they have a fear of punishment.

They may be looking for acceptance through their exaggerations or because they want to draw attention to themselves. They may, on the other hand, be suffering from hereditary spirits of lying or from learned behaviour in the home. Sometimes it can be the parental example of 'Tell them I'm not in' to the window cleaner or to friends whom they don't wish to see and the child soon learns from their example.

Chapter 4

Praying for Healing: Basic Principles

Children will need to feel safe, accepted, and sense that you believe them before they will be confident enough to share with you the deepest fears and the damage within their hearts. It is very important therefore to provide a **safe and secure** setting for prayer ministry times, one preferably which over a period of time they have become used to and feel happy with. A large draughty, spooky church hall or vestry is not really very conducive; neither is their own home necessarily. It may be that that is the very place in which some of the damage has occurred and even though the children may have come from a Christian home, we must never take anything for granted. Just because the parents are Christian, it doesn't mean that nothing bad may have happened there.

Another important principle is to **accept the child** as he is without forming any prior judgements as to what he is like or what has happened. Ask the Lord to give you a love and a compassion for him. It is crucial that you try, at all times, to **always** keep your word. **Trust** will be tremendously important to the child and if you have promised to meet him at a certain time, or take him to a set place, then unless you have a totally unavoidable emergency, you must keep that appointment at all costs. In this area of trust, please remember that it will take time for the child to learn to trust you, and this will be especially true if trust has been fractured by other key figures. Whatever you do, don't force confidences, and please don't say, 'This is our secret,' for others may have said that with dire consequences. Don't put words into their mouths; rather wait until they are ready to share. Don't ask leading questions. Let them tell you in their own words, giving them as much time as they need in order to feel secure and safe.

Take time to build a **good understanding** of the child, remembering that this may involve, depending on their age: playing games, reading stories, going swimming, looking at pictures, drawing, writing, singing, or colouring, in fact anything which will give you an awareness of where the child is. Very often the use of games will help to bring a young child out of a fantasy life into some reality and will help you to understand what is going on in their minds. It has been said that during the last war, adults in England talked incessantly about what was happening in their own neighbourhood and area, whilst the children expressed their fears and anxieties by playing war games first, before eventually they would talk and share.

One of the avenues you will need to explore is that of gaining information about the child and building up a field of **knowledge**. Parents, relatives, and friends will all be helpful here but primarily you will need to get to know the child personally, and allow the child to get to know you. In this area of knowledge we also will be required to teach the child some of the basic facts of the Christian faith. Again we cannot take it for granted that they will have an understanding of the faith, just because they have regularly attended Sunday school. Some of the truths, which they will need to understand, are truths about God: who He is and how He feels about sin. It may be helpful to explore with them what sin is, and how they can deal with their sin and develop a relationship with God. Explain to them who Jesus is, and what He has done for us. The knowledge and language of course, will have to be suited to the age of the child with whom you are praying. This all takes quite a lot of time before we even get to praying for the child, but we must make provision for that time in order to build trust, understanding and knowledge.

Above all develop **patience** and be real with the child for he will soon sound you out. Children can spot a fake a mile off! Be determined to believe the child, for this will be a big issue with them. Someone who has abused them may have convinced them that they will not be believed. Of course you will have to be discerning, but hold an attitude of belief until you have sure and certain evidence to the contrary that they are not telling you the truth.

Keep the prayer ministry time short, remembering that a child's concentration span is fairly limited. This will depend of course on his age. For a young child the time together should probably last no longer than around forty-five minutes all told. This would include taking notes, talking, praying and blessing the child. There is always the exception of course! Don't be longwinded, and be specific in your requests, asking the Lord in short, succinct sentences what you want Him to do for the child. Get rid of any old fashioned words such as 'Thee' and 'Thou', if necessary keeping them for adult praying!

Chapter 5

Praying for Healing: Basic Practices

When you have built up trust, understanding and knowledge of the child in your care, you will then be ready to pray for him. There are a number of basic practices, which you can call upon, and the following are some, which I personally have found very useful.

Laying on of hands

Please ask permission from the child as to whether you can lay your hand upon their shoulder as you pray, as they may have been physically or sexually abused in the past. Be very sensitive. One child automatically flinched away from a prayer ministry person every time they approached them even if they were only going to give them a hug. The preliminary time of talking, sharing and building knowledge and understanding will have given you some insight into where the child is as regards touching their arm or shoulder. We need to respect them in this respect just as we would an adult.

Anointing with oil

It is possible, as when you are praying with an adult, to make use of sanctified oil in prayer times. This can be useful even when praying for little children, as happened recently in the case of a small three-year-old. She had hurt her hand and had asked her mother to pray for Jesus to make it better. The mother asked the child if she would like a little bit of 'Jesus oil' on her palm, to which she replied that she did. For weeks after the incident the child offered the 'Jesus oil' to anyone who was injured, who maybe had a headache or a backache. This didn't matter if it was a close member of the family or a visiting stranger! However just as in the situation of asking permission to lay hands on a child so we must always ask permission in this area of anointing with oil.

Gifts of the Spirit

It is possible, and some people would say vital, to make use of the gifts of the Holy Spirit when praying for children. Words of knowledge, discernment and gifts of healings and miracles are as necessary here as at any other time of praying for others. Don't be frightened to ask the child if anything is happening or whether he has anything he wishes to contribute. Many children will get a picture or tell you that Jesus is saying something to them when you begin to pray. Expect the Holy Spirit to give you words of knowledge or discernment just as He would in the case of an adult, for He has a heart for children.

Ministry of angels

> *'For I tell you that their angels in heaven always see the face of my Father in heaven.'* (Matthew 18:10)

Don't be frightened to ask God to send His angels to minister to the child and to guard them when you leave, especially if there are deep fears or nightmares involved.

Word of God

Make good use of the Scriptures, for the Holy Spirit will often want to apply them to the situation in which you are praying. One eight-year-old girl informed me sadly that she 'was a mistake'. This was something which her mother had laughingly informed her about when the little girl realised that she was the sixth and the last girl in the family. Her parents had wanted a boy and had kept trying to achieve this, only to find that they kept producing girls! Psalm 139 became very meaningful to her as we shared together in prayer that God had put her into her mother's womb, and that He was delighted with her sex.

Name of Jesus

The name of Jesus is also a tremendous weapon in prayer especially in the area of physical healing or the deliverance ministry. This was especially brought home to me when praying for a teenager one evening; he threatened, in a gruff deep voice, that he was about to kill a member of a congregation in the district. After much prayer and deliverance, the powerful name of Jesus silenced that voice and set the young man free.

Chapter 6

Praying for Healing: Ways of Ministering

Whenever you enter prayer ministry times with a child, you need to remember two things. The first is that you need to keep tracing the reasons for the hurt and the damage with which you are dealing, otherwise you will end up simply praying for the symptoms but leaving the roots undealt with. Remember that children's behaviour may be a long way from the root cause of their problem, so don't waste time ministering to the symptoms. Find out the cause, for when that is known it will give direction to your prayers. If you spend some time praying on your own for the child, talking and listening to God, you will be enabled to find out what the child's actual need is. It goes without saying that it is necessary during the prayer ministry time to keep one ear open to the child, whilst at the same time listening to what God is wanting to input through the Holy Spirit.

The second thing, which you need to remember, is that there are different ways of praying for a child. The following are some of the methods which I personally have found quite helpful depending on the situation and the age of the child involved.

Praying over a child whilst he is asleep or unaware

God is a Spirit and He never sleeps, and likewise we too are spirit and our spirit does not sleep either. So it is possible to pray for children whilst they are sleeping, believing that God is able to touch their spirit and bring about the healing that is necessary for them. We can pray either in our own language or in the heavenly language of the Holy Spirit, for we are encouraged to believe from Scripture that He intercedes for us in words that cannot be uttered. He has a heart for, and knows the deepest needs of the child, and we can be sure that He prays through us the perfect prayer and the Father who hears that prayer will answer according to His perfect will.

Praying with the child

If a parent, grandparent, relative, friend or Sunday school teacher is used to praying with the child, then when it comes to praying for deeper issues it will be very natural to them if you suggest praying into these areas. They will see that prayer is very real and meaningful to you, and therefore will become so for them. One mother, who regularly prayed for her children whilst giving them a hug, assumed that they didn't realise what she was doing. She continued the tradition into their teens and was greatly surprised, after hugging and praying for her daughter one day, when the young girl casually inquired of her mother: 'Are you finished yet?'

Get the child's will involved as much as possible, so that they can work with you. It is important, if possible, to get the **parents** involved when you pray, for God especially hears their hearts, as they have certain rights concerning their children. Try to make use of any parental knowledge and concern which they have on behalf of their child and be careful to make sure that they are not supplanted, for they too will be very anxious and hurting. Remember that they are not in competition with you; instead see them as helpers and allies.

Parents are vital to the child and as such they will have lots to contribute. Work with them, and give them their rightful place, always remembering that there is a godly bonding between parent and child which the Lord honours. Try to keep them informed as much as possible, with the consent of the child, always assuming that they are not a part of the problem. If they are then you will have to be very sensitive as to what and how much you share.

It is interesting to see from Scripture that all classes of parents brought their children to Jesus. The rich nobleman who was also a royal official (John 4:47). The ordinary but desperate father of an epileptic boy (Luke 10:37–42). A Gentile mother who was anxious on behalf of her demon-possessed daughter (Matthew 15:26). Jairus who was a ruler of the synagogue (Luke 8:41), and a lonely, grief-stricken widow who was weeping over the death of her only son (Luke 7:11).

It is also true that **all** conditions were brought to Jesus for healing. For example:

- **Those in need of deliverance** were brought to Him, as happened in the situation of the mother with a demonically infested daughter (Matthew 15), and the father who brought his only son to Jesus. The boy had epilepsy, which in this case, although by no means in all, was caused by demonic activity (Luke 9).
- **Those who were dying**: The nobleman's son, who was sick and near death, needed the touch, or in this case the healing word of Jesus (John 4), as did Jairus' daughter who was also near death at the time of her father's request (Luke 8).
- **Those who had died**: The Mother whose only son had died didn't actually bring him to Jesus, but rather Jesus reached out to her in compassion (Luke 7).

Not all of the parents whom you meet will be in the same place of faith or prayer for their child, but again we can take hope and encouragement from the Scriptures. Some parents had faith for their child (the Gentile woman), some heard His word and believed it (the Nobleman), some pleaded persistently for their child (a Gentile woman), some were broken on behalf of their child (the father of the epileptic), and some had almost given up hope (Jairus).

Spiritual warfare

Another method of praying for children is that of speaking into the heavenly places for our children, in other words doing spiritual warfare on their behalf. Paul tells us in Ephesians 6 that we wrestle not against flesh and blood but against principalities and powers. As parents, and those in *loco parentis*, we have an authority in the heavenly realms, and we have the right to come against such strongholds in the name of Jesus on their behalf. It is necessary to be specific and to remember that the demonic activity often gets worse before it gets better. The Holy Spirit will lead you into the particular areas which need prayer, and often talking it over with others who are involved in deliverance ministry will help.

One lady whose son was having difficulty both at home and at school decided to become a governor of the school which her son attended, in order that she would be in a place of legal authority to do spiritual warfare. She felt strongly that his problems were centred in the classroom he was in, so she found out something of the history of the school and prayed accordingly. Satan knows his rights and we need to know ours! After getting the agreement of the head teacher she prayed in the classroom and both her child and the teachers knew the difference.

A teacher has the right to take authority over any disruptive behaviour, rowdiness, etc., in her classroom. If it is of a demonic nature you can take authority in the name of Jesus, and you will also find it beneficial to pray around the classroom using oil that has been sanctified. It may be that you will need to do some spiritual warfare before the class begins. One very disturbed and disruptive child was put into the class of a Christian teacher. After a week she was astonished and disheartened to find that the whole class was in a state of disarray. The other children's education was suffering tremendously, and she herself was coming under severe stress. So in her desperation she prayed and anointed the classroom with oil, taking her authority as one that was in *loco parentis*. She bound the enemy and refused to let him operate in her classroom. To her amazement the prayer worked! It was only the following year, after he moved into the next class, that the extremely disruptive behaviour started again. Some of the areas you may need to pray into are: victim spirits, bullying, disruption, taunting, etc., It is also helpful to break any ungodly soul ties between antagonists or cohorts! Pray the peace and blessing of Jesus into your classroom also.

Some parents have even begun prayer support groups for the schools which their children attend and have noted tremendous differences. In this area of spiritual warfare the ability to be able to bind and loose the enemy is the key, and as Christians we have that right. We also have the right to ask the Lord to send the Holy Spirit on our own and on our children's behalf.

Intercession

I very strongly believe that intercession is one of the major keys in setting children free from pain and hurt and bringing them into wholeness. Lamentations 3:48 asserts:

> *'Streams of tears flow from my eyes because my people are destroyed.'*

Those tears, which are shed in prayer, for little ones and young people, are very precious in the Lord's sight. Satan hates to see us on our knees for children, whether they are our own or those whom God has lain upon our hearts. We need to learn how to 'take hold of God's coat-tails' and not to let Him go until He answers us.

Beryl Burgess has written an excellent book in this whole area of intercession, giving the Body of Christ some very important clues as how to be effective in this vital ministry. It is called *Dear Mark and Sarah* (published by New Wine Press), and is a series of letters explaining how she sets about praying for children. Briefly the following seems to be her method. Usually Beryl does not meet the children for whom she prays, but simply gathers as much information as she can from those who know the child: its parents, relatives, and friends. She then adds to her knowledge information from her own experience of childhood as well as her knowledge of other young children. She then asks the Holy Spirit how she should pray.

She prays through the child's life, beginning with his conception, through his birth, his life as a toddler, through his school life and as a teenager, until his present age. Beryl uses concentration aids to help her to focus in prayer. For instance, she prays aloud and often asks another person to help her in her intercession, for there is power in the agreement between two people. The intercession time will usually last about two hours. She gets reports on the progress of the child from the parents and usually prays into the chief trouble spot first and deals with that. She finds that accompanying difficulties will often clear up. She prays into blocks of three years at a time and has found that shock often seems to be the start of many problems. She prays the negative out and the positive in, finding out from Holy Spirit any specific areas of physical, emotional or spiritual wounding which needs dealing with. I recommend this book highly to those of you who feel called into the ministry of intercession on behalf of children. It will be an invaluable tool in your hands for setting children free.

Chapter 7

Praying for Healing: Special Needs

Praying for the unborn child

From the moment of conception damage may have been inflicted upon the child, especially if it was conceived during casual sex, in an incestuous relationship, or through anger or rape. If the child has been conceived in any of these circumstances it is probable that the mother will also have been very damaged. This will most likely have had an out-working upon the child. Her fear, anger and shock may have been transferred into the spirit of the child and may also have caused deep emotional pain. Pray against any consequential damage, asking the Lord to feed His love and comfort into the child, lifting off any fear and insecurity. The child may also feel starved inside their spirit and they will need to have prayer into this area too. The Holy Spirit, the Comforter, can reach into the innermost part of the child in the womb and bring His warmth and comfort into their young spirit.

Many children are living in rejection because of such input into their very early beginnings. In such children there will most likely be a root of a lack of a sense of their own worth and self-esteem. I have found it very helpful to minister in, or to get the mother to pray in, the truth of Psalm 139, which speaks of the Lord knowing each of us from the moment of our conception. This can be very healing for both the mother and the child.

In a normal pregnancy the parents can speak words of acceptance and encouragement over the child in the womb, assuring them of their love and delight in the forthcoming birth. The mother and father can pray against any known defect that may be in the family line as well as any known generational sins. I include in the Appendix an anonymous mother's experience of praying through the nine months prior to her baby's birth, which may be of some help to you. If anyone knows the origins I would gladly give credit for it.

Praying for the sexually abused

It will be essential to spend much time with the child talking, sharing, and bringing out into the open the trauma of the abuse, before you begin any prayer ministry whatsoever. You will need to build up a position of trust and belief that will enable the child, however young or old, to share with you the deepest parts of his or her inner being.

If a child or a young person has been sexually abused there will inevitably be deep damage to their inner being. Their emotions will be in a state of serious conflict. They will probably experience a mixture of feelings: anger, guilt, shame, fear and confusion. Maybe they will feel ambivalent towards the person who has abused them, since this is a person who is normally well-known to them.

They will need to express their true feelings in the safety of a loving, believing and accepting atmosphere, and it is perhaps unnecessary to stress that confidentiality is of prime importance. It may take them a long while, but they will need to come to the position of choosing to forgive the one who abused them, realising that this may take much longer than we would realise. There will most likely be a whole series of people whom they will need to forgive: parents for not seeing what was happening; God for not stopping it and themselves for allowing it to happen (even though they probably had little choice).

The sexual act is meant to be a godly one of joining together, in the safety of marriage, two people into a one-flesh relationship. Unfortunately what God meant for good, Satan tries to use for evil and in an ungodly union there is still that joining together of two people, however old or young they may be. It will be necessary, therefore, when praying for children or young people in the area of sexual abuse, to break any ungodly bonding between the abuser and the abused.

Most people who have been sexually abused usually feel very ashamed and they carry around with them a sense of being dirty. Ask Jesus to come and cleanse them in the water of the Holy Spirit; to put them under His waterfall and bring them complete cleansing. Depending on the age of the child you will need to address any demonic spirits which are present in language which is relevant and acceptable to them. For example, with a small child you could ask Jesus to lift off any bad thing that may have come to them through the abuse, whilst with a young person you could actually address the demonic more directly. However, be careful what language you use as both children and young people have very vivid imaginations. The enemy knows what you mean and he will have to obey you because of your authority in Jesus.

Because of the sexual act there will have been a joining of body, soul and spirit, and in some cases the abuse can be so bad that there will be a fracture, a breaking as it were between the body and the spirit. Minister into, and pray for the Lord to integrate the spirit, soul and body of the person, asking that He will bring the person into a place of wholeness and unity.

Praying for the adopted or fostered child

It may be that the child you are praying for has been born as a result of sexual sin; maybe it has been conceived out of wedlock, and if that is so, then you will need to break the curse of Deuteronomy 23:2 over them. If the child is old enough to understand what you are doing and is able to receive such knowledge, it will be very helpful to them if you share what you are doing and why you are doing it. Otherwise break the curse quietly but surely before the Lord, knowing that He will hear you on behalf of the child.

Very often such children have no protective walls around them and they will have come into the world deeply wounded. It is most likely that they will have felt rejection whilst in the womb or shortly after their birth. Serious rejection is often written deeply into the heart of the adopted child and they will need the Lord to bind up their broken hearts.

Such children may begin to have an identity crisis in their teenage years. They may develop a great need to find their birth parents and they will often test the adopted or fostered parents, pushing them as far as they will go. In this area of identity it is good and necessary to address and pray into any confusion of identity which the child may feel and call forth the real person. Sometimes an adopted child needs to be called out of the shadows into his own place, for he may have hidden his true identity through shame and for his own security.

He or she may have become performance orientated, having a need to please others in order to be accepted and they also may have developed a fear of intimate relationships. Speak rest, trust and belonging into them and keep praying into the rejection areas, doing both inner healing and deliverance as and when you discern them to be necessary.

Praying for the wounded spirit

If a child has a wounded spirit, you will need to determine the cause of the wounding, in other words to look for the root. For example if a child has a crushed spirit, you will go through the interview session, trying to discern how and why that has come about. For example, it may be that the child's parents were very strict and controlling and very disapproving. This may have resulted in the child becoming very crushed and wounded in his spirit, in which case you will need to break ungodly bonding with his parents and pray the Holy Spirit's comfort and strength into him. Take time to build up and nurture the child's spirit and teach him how to renew his mind and give his thoughts to Jesus.

If the child has an imprisoned spirit, you will again need to look for the root. Maybe they experienced a very difficult trauma whilst in the womb and that has resulted in his spirit becoming bound and imprisoned. Minister into these areas under the direction of the Holy Spirit, feeding and nurturing his spirit. For more help in praying into the human spirit, you may find it helpful to refer to my book, *Healing the Human Spirit*.

Praying into various conditions

Dyslexia

Children with dyslexia seem to have a communication disorder and one of the keys, which you may wish to try, is that off lifting off a curse of 'word blindness' on the generational line. If the child is old enough there may also need to be repentance for blindness to God's word, generationally.

Physical

Before praying for the child's physical complaints you will need to discern whether the condition is simply physical, or whether the physical is caused by an emotional or spiritual cause. Ask the Lord for discernment as to whether there are any spirits of infirmity present, and address them in appropriate language if that is so.

However, if it is straightforward case of praying for physical healing, then take your courage in both hands and reach out in faith on behalf of the child. The Lord has a compassionate heart and longs to answer such prayers. One day a teacher called a little boy in her class to her desk to read for her. His hands were all covered with warts and he was very ashamed and embarrassed about them. Usually he hid them in his pockets. On this day however, he inadvertently put them on her desk whilst he was reading. She felt such a compassion for him that she gently touched his hands and silently asked Jesus to heal them. Next day his hands were clear. He was absolutely delighted, telling all of his friends: 'It's a miracle – the warts just went in the night.'

Anorexia and bulimia

This is a complex area and needs much discernment as to the root of the eating disorder, before beginning to pray into it. There was a report in *The Times* newspaper on November 28th 1997 concerning the work of Dr Dee Dawson, medical director of the Rhodes Farm Clinic in North London, which treats children with eating disorders, which made very interesting reading. She felt that anorexics tended to be obsessive, compulsive perfectionists who would rip up work until they were satisfied. She blamed low-fat diets, modern exercise regimes and the trend towards vegetarianism for many eating disorders. She believed that it was no coincidence that 80 per cent of her patients were vegetarian. This is not to plead against the vegetarian case but rather to point out that eating disorders are a very complex subject.

There are many and varied reasons for these conditions and the following are some, which we have found to be fairly common: perfectionism, guilt, shock, an expectation to perform, a fear of failure, rebellion and control. Therefore when praying into this condition, as with all of the others, it is especially important to find out what is the root. For example, two girls presented themselves for ministry both with an anorexic condition. One girl developed anorexia in her teens, because she was terrified of becoming a woman. This was due to a fear of the sexual act, which she had been forced to observe whilst a very young girl. I have already related to you the story of the other young girl who was forced to eat rice pudding, whilst being sick at the same time. She never forgot that incident and the hatred of her father became tied in with her developing hatred of food. It was only when the couple praying for her discerned this situation, that the ministry began to be effective. It would have been useless to minister to the first girl in the same manner as they ministered to the second, for the unique root of each had to be discerned and dealt with on an individual basis.

Praying for deliverance

In deliverance ministry it is important to listen to the child and to the parents as to what the problem is, when it began and whether anyone else in the family, either present day or in the past, has suffered in a similar manner. It is also absolutely necessary to listen to the Holy Spirit. If a young child has its parent present then involve them and explain what you are doing. If it is an older child you are praying for then you can ask the child questions as to how they are feeling during the time together. Watch the body language of parents and child and the interaction between them. Be discerning as to what is happening, and don't forget to pray protection for the child and its family as well as yourself and your family. Bind the enemy and using language in keeping with the age of the child, ask Jesus to lift the bad things away that are causing the nightmares, the bad thoughts and the bad feelings, etc.

There was one little boy, who was brought for prayer by his mother. He had a great fear which centred on the possibility of his mum and dad having a terrible accident. We spent a great deal of time sharing about his fear, when it had started and what it felt like. Eventually we discerned the fear was both emotional and demonic, so we talked about Jesus looking after his mum and dad and in prayer we asked Jesus to take away the fear and lift away anything which was making him fearful. Later in his own home he told his parents: 'I'm not going to worry any more for I know now that Jesus will look after you.' The emotional and the demonic were dealt with very simply and the Lord heard that innocent prayer on behalf of the child. After doing deliverance ministry please remember to ask Jesus to fill the child with His Holy Spirit. With very young children I would tend to pray for deliverance for them whilst they are asleep.

Praying for children in our care

School teachers, Sunday school teachers, youth workers and any others who have a care for children, all have a very important role in the lives of the children whom they look after and they can do much to pray for them in different situations. Whilst remembering the damage which can be done to children and the great need that there is to intercede for them, it is always important to remember that praying for their salvation is prime. Remember that the age of accountability is probably much younger than we would think, and that children can receive Christ at a very early age. Teach the Gospel to them very simply, telling them about God, sin, Jesus, and salvation. When you counsel for salvation keep the vocabulary as understandable as possible. Dialogue with the children but don't preach to them. It is sometimes effective to use one Bible verse and to press the truth home with that, rather than use a number and therefore run the risk of becoming confusing. Children will also value the use of songs, drama, visual aids, and quizzes if possible. Do encourage the child to respond, and without any undue pressure, offer to pray with them for salvation. Remember also to pray for the child to be filled with the Holy Spirit.

It will also be necessary to find someone who will be willing to nurture the new life, always remembering that the child is still a child. Don't expect too much but keep watching for growth in the spiritual life and encourage it where possible. Maybe it would be good to have a number of senior members of the congregation committed to praying regularly for each child in the church or Sunday school. The parents or Sunday school teachers could pass confidential information on to them so that they could pray intelligently.

In one instance of this happening, one young boy was having difficulty because he was being bullied at school, and the situation was transformed once the 'senior prayer' was informed and went to work in prayer! If you can get each child covered in prayer, then God will honour that for He sees that you are taking seriously His Son's admonition:

> *'Let the little children come to me, and do not hinder them, for the Kingdom of God belongs to such as these.'*
>
> (Luke 18:16)

Be prepared to pray for the child (with the parents' consent) if they are in need of healing for any of the above areas which we have been speaking about: abuse, adoption, deliverance, spiritual or emotional pain.

A prayer for children in our care

The following is a prayer that I have sometimes used for the children within my care, either as a parent, a Sunday school teacher, a secular teacher or a youth worker. Usually I would be praying without the children in my presence.

'Lord Jesus, we acknowledge Your presence. We welcome the Holy Spirit. We bless You and thank You for the children in our care. We stand now before You on their behalf. We thank You for the godly bonding which we have with them. We ask You now by the power of Your Holy Spirit to find these children wherever they are, and begin to lift off them any damage which the enemy has inflicted upon them. We stand in the gap and confess any hurt, pain or sin that has been done to them through other human beings. We seek forgiveness and cleansing on their behalf. We take our authority in Christ and bind the enemy in their lives, especially in the life of .... [name]. We ask You, Heavenly Father, to lift off the enemy's footprints and pour Your blessings upon them. We ask You now to bring to our mind any particular needs which we need to pray for, in Jesus' Name.'

(At this point I would wait upon the Holy Spirit for direction, words of knowledge and wisdom and pray accordingly.)

Chapter 8

Praying for Healing:
Family Dynamics

Up to this point we have been considering in what ways a child, as an individual, can be hurt and wounded and thus suffer much damage. However it is also good and in fact essential to remember, that whilst you may be praying for a child in isolation, nevertheless he is a part of a much larger structure which you will need to be aware of, and be willing to take into account for future action. It is no help to the child if you bring him to a place of healing, only to send him back into the family unit which may be contributing to the hurt and pain from which he has just been set free.

It is true with the family unit, as it is with the individual, that our enemy Satan is seeking to rob and destroy and cause damage here too. This is nothing new, for from the very beginning he has sought to attack and demolish the family. The story of Adam and Eve and their two sons Cain and Abel demonstrate this admirably, for this first family was devastated and destroyed by Satan, with one son being murdered and the other one being the murderer. God Himself had warned Cain that *'sin is crouching at your door'* (Genesis 4:7), but Cain ignored God's advice and plunged right into his sin.

Family therapy would instance a number of situations which are harmful to the family unit functioning well and it is very interesting that we can see many of these situations at work within the Scriptures. For example, some of these areas would be the breakdown of inter-personal relationships: marital conflict, sibling rivalry, family conflict, scape-goating and strife. The Scriptures are full of incidents of family hurt and pain and they give a very good description of these dynamics, which go on within the family unit.

For example we could instance the story of Abraham, Sarah and Isaac in Genesis chapters 16–21, for they tell the story of the family conflict between Sarah, Hagar and their two sons Isaac and Ishmael. Two children from different mothers, but with the same father, is still the recipe today for difficulties and conflict if not confronted in the right way. There was an intense jealousy between the two women and this can still happen in second parent families. It can give rise to an atmosphere of resentment, abandonment, rejection, anger, grief, and fear. To minister and to pray for the 'Ishmael' in the family and then send him back into the same family atmosphere could court disaster and undo all the good praying which has taken place.

Genesis chapters 24–28 go on to talk of the family difficulties of Isaac and Rebekah with all of the built-in family conflict. The mother, who favoured the youngest son, actually stirs up Jacob and Esau in their conflict. She encourages her favourite boy Jacob to deceive his father and try to get his blessing. So we have a family where the wife deceives her husband, the son deceives his father and the eldest son becomes angry and eventually separated from the family unit. We see here the isolation of one or the other spouse; favouritism within the family unit, as well as much deception at work. One lady, for whom we prayed, had formed an incestuous relationship with her eldest son; this was not sexual bonding but rather an emotional joining. Nevertheless it had a devastating effect upon the family unit, and to pray for the boy without dealing with the family dynamics would have been virtually ineffectual, as the situation to which he was returning was unchanged.

In the area of family conflict the story of Jacob, Rachel and Leah is also very enlightening (Genesis 29–35). We see here a prime example of marital discord within the home, where the husband prefers one wife (Rachel) above another (Leah). Fortunately today we live in a monogamous society, but the same dynamics can be seen to be at work, where a second spouse feels displaced by a mistress or a second partner. Often there will be intense jealousy and rivalry between them and any of their offspring.

Genesis chapters 37–47 relates a story of what could be modern-day scape-goating: the story of Joseph and his elder brothers. The conflict centred on the brother's jealousy of the youngest favoured son. Joseph was evidently quite spoilt by his father, who aggravated the situation by buying him the beautiful multi-coloured coat. In the end jealousy won out and Joseph was made to carry all of the pain and all of the frustration of the family. He became the scapegoat.

To pray for the scapegoat in the family, without being aware as to the family dynamics, would be very unwise, for any favouritism, unless dealt with, will continue to give rise to a pecking order, and rejection will again take root. 'The black sheep of the family' will continue to take the flak.

The family of King David is also a very interesting one and to observe the dynamics between King David the father and his son Absalom tells you a lot about inter-personal relationships. Here we have a modern-day situation of a son trying to usurp the authority of the father. To do a study of the relationships between David and his other children is also enlightening. For example, Amnon, David's son and Tamar his daughter, had an incestuous relationship, whilst the relationship between Absalom and Amnon left a lot to be desired. In fact in the end one brother murders another! Truly they could be described as a dysfunctional family.

Today we see many families where there is hatred amongst siblings, where there is sexual abuse in evidence and rebellion against the parents. To return a child to such an atmosphere without being aware of what is happening is very short-sighted and can be distinctly harmful.

So we can see that ministering to a child as an individual, in isolation, will do some good but for greater effect one must take into account the dynamics of the family in which he lives. It is helpful to know whether there is any **scapegoating** going on or any **marital discord**. What is happening in the areas of **sibling rivalry** and **inter-personal relationships**? Are the relationships healthy? I have sometimes found it helpful, in order to get a clearer picture of the family atmosphere surrounding a child, to do a family worksheet. This helps you to form a picture as to what the family unit (from which the child comes and to which he will be returning) looks like. With such knowledge you can pray intelligently and maybe prepare the family and the child as much as possible, for future health and well-being. I enclose a copy in the Appendix, which you may find useful.

Praying for the individual child and working within the family unit will do much to not only set the child free, but will also enable him to continue to walk into the freedom, which Jesus died to give him. The Lord has a heart for His little ones and His invitation to *'Suffer the little children to come unto me'* still stands, but the question remains, 'Who will bring them?' My prayer is that the reader of this book will be inspired to continually seek and to search out the lost for Him, however young or broken they may be.

Appendix 1

A mother's prayers, thoughts and words for her baby in the womb

Conception

> *'Before I was born the Lord called me; from my birth he has made mention of my name.'* (Isaiah 49:1)

Hear Him call your name; you are chosen.

First month

> *'You knit me together in my mother's womb.'*
> (Psalm 139:13)

His presence covered you in your mother's womb.

Second month

> *'Before you were born I set you apart; I appointed you as a prophet to the nations.'* (Jeremiah 1:5)

God approved of you and is happy with your sexual identity.

Third month

> *'I praise you because I am fearfully and wonderfully made.'*
> (Psalm 139:14)

Praise God for the miracle of your creation.

Fourth month

> *'In the sight of God, who gives life to everything.'*
> (1 Timothy 6:13)

God quickened you and gave you life. Thank Him.

Fifth month

> *'There is no fear in love. But perfect love drives out fear.'*
> (1 John 4:18)

If you felt your mother's fears, receive healing. Thank God for your mother and life and nourishment received through her.

Sixth month

> *'The baby in my womb leaped for joy.'*   (Luke 1:44)

You were anointed top to toe with protective ointment (*Vernix caseosa*) and spiritually you are anointed.

Seventh month

> *'My frame was not hidden from you when I was made in the secret place. When I was woven together in the depths of the earth, your eyes saw my unformed body.'*   (Psalm 139:15)

By the middle of this month all parts of your body are completed. God is preparing you for birth.

Eighth month

> *'You will nurse and be carried on her arm and dandled on her knees.'*   (Isaiah 66:12)

God's presence is there; He's getting you and your mother ready for the process of birth.

Ninth month

> *'A woman giving birth to a child has pain because her time has come; but when her baby is born she forgets the anguish because of her joy that a child is born into the world.'*
>
> (John 16:21)

As you move out of the dark birth canal, the light of Jesus draws you to Him. He delivers you, cleans you up and presents you to His Father.

Appendix 2

FATHER'S
PAIN

**FAMILY
DYNAMICS**

MOTHER'S
PAIN

FAMILY
ATMOSPHERE

GENERATIONAL
PAIN

OWN
PAIN

SIBLING'S
PAIN